POWER

To Magnitise

Money and Reject

POVERTY

Dr. D. K. Olukoya

POWER TO MAGNETISE MONEY
AND REJECT POVERTY
© 2012 DR. D. K. OLUKOYA
ISBN: 978-978-920-021-4
Published - May 2012 AD

Published by:
The Battle Cry Christian Ministries

322, Herbert Macaulay Street, Sabo, Yaba
P. O. Box 12272, Ikeja, Lagos
www.battlecryng.com
email: sales@battlecryng.com
Phone: 0803-304-4239, 01-8044415

I Salute my wonderful wife, Pastor Shade, for her invaluable support in the ministry.
I appreciate her unquantifiable support in the book ministry
as the cover designer, art editor and art adviser.

All the scriptures are from the King James Version.

TABLE OF CONTENTS

CHAPTER ONE

POWER
TO MAGNETISE
MONEY AND
REJECT
POVERTY

Matthew 17:24-27 says:

> *And when they were come to Capernaum, they that received tribute money came to Peter, and said, Doth not your master pay tribute? He saith, Yes. And when he was come into the house, Jesus prevented him, saying, What thinkest thou, Simon? of whom do the kings of the earth take custom or tribute? of their own children, or of strangers? Peter saith unto him, of strangers. Jesus saith unto him, Then are the children free. Notwithstanding, lest we should offend them, go thou to the sea, and cast an hook, and take up the fish that first cometh up; and when thou hast opened his mouth, thou shalt find a piece of money: that take, and give unto them for me and thee.*

The King who has the ability to convert the mouth of a fish to a bank is the God we serve. I decree that the evil mouth speaking against your promised land shall be silenced by fire, in the name of Jesus.

This shows why money flows to some Christians and flows away from others. One first lesson you must learn is that money flows. It can flow away from a person. It can be magnetised or repelled.

AN UNFORGETTABLE EXPERIENCE

Many year ago, my father, who has gone to be with the Lord now, one day came to the football field where I was playing football, beckoned to me and said, "Daniel, come out." I came out and he said, "Jump into the car." I jumped into the car. I asked him where we were going but he didn't answer. He drove me straight to the church. It was a Saturday evening and I knew that there was no service on Saturday evening. When we got there he held my hand and took me inside the auditorium of the church where a choir practice was going on. He called the choir master and told him to write my name in the choir, that he preferred me to be singing in the choir than to be playing in that football field.

I was very unhappy because as I looked around the place 99 per cent of the people were women. But looking back now I thank him most sincerely for dumping me there. When I got there that day, they were taking new people in the choir. They were testing their voices. A lady called Jolomi was tested and she sang very poorly. The choir master tried to make her improve but it was a futile effort. After sometime the choir master looked at her and said, "My sister, you like the choir but the choir does not like you."

This is the same thing with money. A lot of people like money, but it flows away.

THE MAGNETS

The ability of a believer to magnetise or repel money is influenced by four main things.

1. Your habit.
2. Your attitude towards money.
3. Your action.
4. Your mentality or belief system.

There are positive magnets and negative magnets. The positive magnets would draw good things to you while the negative would push them away from you.

Many years ago, there was a woman in this ministry who sold food in a primary school. It was a large school and there were 14 food sellers. This woman was poor and each day she came back home with three-quarters of the rice and beans unsold. Every night she would eat some of the unsold food until the children began to complain that they ate rice and beans every night. She was cooking at a loss and by the time she came to me for counselling, I asked her whether other women were selling their food easily and she said, "Yes, the students just go to them, but something seems to be chasing them away from my food."

ANGELS OF PROSPERITY

Beloved the truth of the matter is that there are angels of prosperity. There are also angels of poverty. They can work for or against a person. By the time this woman prayed and anointed where she was selling her food, the students moved over to her. Declare this loud and clear: "Angels of poverty, my life is not your candidate, go away, in the name of Jesus.

I learnt a strange lesson in 1985. It was in Abuja. Before she got married, this sister had three houses and four cars. She had worked hard as a lawyer. Then around the age of 34 or 35 she got married. Five months after the wedding the couple were borrowing to eat. The houses and cars were gone. When they came for counselling. I said, "Let us pray" and all of us joined hands and I started to pray. All of a sudden, a roaring voice spoke in Yoruba: "Emini emere alakisa (I am the family spirit with rags). I was surprised because I heard that for the first time. Then I asked the spirit what its agenda was. It laughed and said it was to turn a good land to a desert. The sister was shaking like a banana leaf. There are powers whose duty it is to grab a fertilised garden and convert it to a desert of woe and poverty. There are some familiar spirits that transfer poverty. May they never gain access to your destiny, in the name of Jesus. If they have gained access, may they be buried alive, in the name of Jesus.

REPELLING FORCES

There are certain things that repel money or push away wealth.

1. **Curses and satanic covenants.** A curse can repel wealth from somebody.
2. **Demonic yokes.** A yoke could be upon a person saying that this is how far he can go, that he cannot go further.
3. **Prayerlessness.** Prayer warriors are never broke unless they are not praying with righteousness. All the prayer warriors in the Scripture were never broke.
4. **Wrong decisions.** If you take a wrong decision, it is a bad investment.
5. **Laziness.**
6. **Bad management of time.**
7. **Bad management of talent.**
8. **Bad management of the money you have.**
9. **Bad management of your opportunities.**
10. **Bad management of human resources.**
11. **Pride.**
12. **Lack of wisdom.**
13. **Lack of creativity.**
14. **A life of sin.** A sinner is doing himself or herself a lot of harm. The Bible says, "A sinner doeth much evil." One sinner in the boat of your life can be the one to cause you a lot of trouble.

15. **Unfriendly attitude.**
16. **Stinginess.** When you are stingy, money runs away from you. The Bible says: "There is he that giveth liberally and he gets plenty. There is he that witholdeth much more than he should only be lead to poverty."
17. **Greed and covetousness.**

I pray that if there is any of these things in your life, may the good Lord help you today to uproot them from your destiny, in the name of Jesus.

One truth you need to know is that the Bible says, "A man shall receive nothing except he be given from above." Whatever the heavens have not put in your hands will not prosper in your hands. That's why if you go to a demon to get money, by the time it does a round-about turn you would have a serious trouble, for the devil does not have any free gift. He operates a primitive trade by batter. That's why when some people who have acquired money from the devil get born, again the first thing God does is to remove that satanic wealth. He would turn them upside down and empty them very well. Then He would now begin to bring His own wealth to them.

The other time I met a man whom I felt like taking a stick and hitting on the head. He said: "Man of God, what kind of deliverance can I do now? I don't think there can be deliverance for me because I killed my own mother to make money, and now I have the money but cannot sleep." His head was as hot as a plugged electric iron. He said he no longer needed the money. The devil has no free gifts at all.

POWERFUL MAGNETS
What are the things that magnetise money?

1. **God's gifts to you.** When you prayerfully develop gifts with training and studying, they become marketable skills. I prophecy to your life that your gifts will change your family history, in the name of Jesus.
2. **Your vision.** By this we mean your mission on earth, the kind of dream you have, your purpose and your assignment. Your divinely-given vision will bring you divine provision. When you have no

vision you cannot make real progress in life.

3. **Creative ideas.** Creative ideas have the capacity to solve problems for you. The enemy knows that once you have creative ideas, that others don't have, they will bring you money. What he now does is to block them. Some people will see themselves doing things in the dream which they find that they are unable to do in real life. Those things have been blocked. I pray that the gap between what God wants you to be and where you are now will be closed by fire, in the name of Jesus.

4. **Services and products that meet the real needs of people.** A believer does not open a shop and just start selling anything there. He needs to prayerfully know what would meet the needs of people and the Lord would lead him as he does so.

5. **Important information.** They say that the best man is the man with the best information and the most successful man is the man with the most useful information. When you come to the church, get information. That's why you find that people of destiny always try and take some notes because they know that the faintest ink is better than the best brain.

6. **Being close to or relating with high quality people.**

7. **Knowledge of regular confession of the word of God.** It is written, "The word of God is quick and powerful, sharper than any two-edged sword." It also says, "This book of the law shall not depart from thy mouth, but thou shall meditate therein day and night." It also says that whosoever delights in the law of God and meditates in His law day and night, whatsoever he does shall prosper. Unfortunately, many Christians are very poor readers of the Bible and fewer number of them memorise the Scriptures. One great thing you can do to your life is to memorise Bible passages. This is an area of weakness of many Christians. Many who come of our meetings do not read their Bible. The only book some have are prayer books.

That is not good enough. Even your prayers should be backed up with Scriptures because the time the devil faced Jesus, He said, "It is written." That "it is written" was an arrow fired into the liver of the devil. I pray that the evil birds that steal the word of God from the hearts of people will not come to your door, in the name of Jesus. It is easy for many people to remember all the names of members of the Super Eagles football team, but if you ask them to tell you the names of the 12 disciples of Jesus they don't know. People in the dark world use incantations. They use tongue soaked in concoction to withdraw other people's prosperity to themselves. As Christians, we have greater power. But why are we not using it? God will help us, in Jesus' name.

8. **The anointing of the Holy Spirit.** I pray that the anointing for prosperity will fall upon you, in the name of Jesus.
9. **Smart work.** Not only must we work hard, we need to work very well. Use your strength and use your sense. The job that gives you the highest level of joy is the one that will give you the highest pay.
10. **Supernatural favour.** Favour is an attractive force given by God that causes us to be approved by men, even men who hate us. It is an invisible spiritual currency that brings earthly currency to us without struggling for it.

11. **Uncommon wisdom.** This will cause you to be creative, innovative, and have marketable ideas. I pray that it comes upon your life, in the name of Jesus.

12. **Divinely ordained projects.** You pray and God says, "Go ahead, this will attract money to you."

13. **Sacrificial giving.** Givers get, while keepers lose. You can therefore attract money by giving and repel poverty. By giving you can release material and financial productivity into your life. That's why the Bible says, "Give and it shall be given unto you." The reverse is true: "Refuse to give and it shall not be given unto you."

Prayer Points

1. I reject every spirit of seduction, in the name of Jesus.

2. I refuse to let sin have dominion over me, in the name of Jesus.

3. I reject every satanic promise in any department of my life, in the name of Jesus.

4. Let the powers setting themselves up in opposition to me be paralysed, in the name of Jesus.

5. O Lord, cancel the effect of all former satanic benefits in my life, in the name of Jesus.
6. You spirit of anger in my life, I bind you, in the name of Jesus.
7. Lord, fill me with strength to replace weakness.
8. Let all spiritual contamination be washed away by the blood of Jesus.
9. Let the cleansing and healing waters of the Lord flow into my life now, in the name of Jesus.
10. Father, I surrender to You today with all my heart and soul, in the name of Jesus.
11. Lord, come into my life in a deeper way.
12. I say yes to You today, O Lord.
13. I open all the secret places of my heart to You, Lord Jesus. Come in.
14. I surrender every department of my life to You, O Lord, in the name of Jesus.
15. I surrender my past, present and future to You, O Lord.

CHAPTER TWO

MOVING TO THE TOP

G od has not destined you for poverty. He has not destined the second place for anyone. He desires that we occupy the first and the best place. However, almost the entire humanity lives in the second place of life. This is very tragic indeed. The average man develops only 10 per cent of his talents before he dies.

God has a good plan for you. You must move up. Do not settle for less. The child of a king is not meant to be feeding from the dustbin. When things go very rough you should know that perhaps you are in the wrong place. Do not be satisfied with where you are now. Make up your mind to run away from every low land because the second place is for losers. The low land is for losers.

THE LEADERS

All the houses in this world belong to only 15 per cent of the people. Research has shown that if you take all the money in the world and distribute it equally to everybody, very soon it will come back to the hands of 15 per cent. it would therefore appear as if there were some people that have been programmed for the bottom. Such people would be experiencing bitterness. Their lives would be falling apart and they would always be angry. They will be demonstrating hatred towards others, would be going from one sickness to the other and would be talking and thinking about giving up. They are nervous and they may even backslide completely and fall away from the faith.

They are the kind of people who will say, "Well, nobody cares about me or my problems." Some will say: "Well, I don't like what is happening to me. Therefore, I won't do anything." It is good for us to consider the habits of those who are programmed for the bottom.

Deuteronomy 28:13 says:

> *And the LORD shall make thee the head, and not the tail; and thou shalt be above only, and thou shalt not be beneath; if that thou hearken unto the commandments of the LORD thy God, which I command thee this day, to observe and to do them.*

Here, two positions are identified straightaway: the head and the tail; above and bottom or beneath. In life there can be only four positions. There is the head, the middle, the bottom and the zero point. The zero point is for those who are dead.

When you talk about the head, it is an important organ of the body. As a servant of God I have seen so many things. I have seen somebody with no legs or hands who was still living. I have seen somebody whose intestine has been taken out and he was still living. I have even seen somebody whose throat has been removed and he could not talk but yet he was still alive. But I am yet to sees somebody whose head has been taken off and he is still living.

THE HEAD
Your head contains the brain, nose, mouth, tongue, ears, eyes and teeth. It contains the computer that runs the whole body and is always at the top. Therefore, God says there is a position called the head. But there is another one called the tail. It is closer to the anus. Unlike the head which has defense weapon (the teeth), there is no teeth in the tail. It can be cut off from an

animal without any serious consequence. This is why some people are unjustly manipulated and nothing happens. The fact that the Bible says "I shall make thee the head and not the tail," shows that those two position are available. But the programme of God for our lives is to make us the head and also to be above. But that God's promise is conditional.

CHARACTERISTICS OF THE POVERTY STRICKEN

1. **Living in the past:** This is called rear mirror syndrome.
2. **Having no purpose at all in life.** This is why we keep telling those who are not yet married to first of all identify their purpose so that they would not marry someone who will defeat their purpose.
3. **Bad time managers:** They don't know how to handle the time in their hands. They let the time control them. Sometimes the dividing line between success and failure is how you manage your time. They say fools waste money but the greatest fools waste time.

4. **Not willing to pay the price of success:** They just want to attain success without suffering or going to any school of affliction. This kind of people will eventually land at the bottom.

5. **Inability to keep relationship with people.** They don't get along with other people.

6. **They stop growing:** Have you learnt anything new this year, or are you just the narrow minded type?. As a Christian are you growing old in the Lord? A person can stay long in the church and still remain a spiritual baby.

7. **Having the loser attitude:** When a person is poverty-stricken, the first habits you will find in his life is that he posseses a negative attitude. He looks at everything in a negative way. He would not know that the negative attitude determines the outcome of much of his situation. It is true that we may not be able to control what happens to us sometimes, but we can choose our response to them. That is why they say that it is the same sun that melts the candle that hardens the clay. Are you always looking at the negative side of things? You must change.

8. **Inability to recognise weaknesses and deal with them:** The Almighty knows that everyone has

weaknesses but the trouble is that one simple weakness can destroy you, if you refuse to recognise it and deal with it. When you don't recognise your dormant weakness, it will schedule you for a trauma you can avoid. That weakness in your life is like a living person, a living organism with you. You must identify it, bring it out and kill it. It is a force, a silent and deadly enemy which if ignored, can wreck your dream completely. It can sabotage all the good things God has planned for your life. The greatest trouble with weaknesses is that they are entry points into your life for demon spirits.

9. **Not seeing their bodies as temples of God:** They misuse their bodies. They commit sins with their bodies and afterwards they start looking for deliverance.

10. **Being never contented:** They live a discontented life. Being contented means you have an inner peace no matter what your circumstances are. Those who are programmed for the bottom are never contented materially. It is sad but true, that most people still believe that money brings

happiness. It is a lie

11. **Hating to experience hardship or pain:** They just want everything to go smoothly.

12. **Always getting worried:** They cultivate the habit of worry, not knowing that worry is a total waste of time. It will give you something to do but will not get you anywhere. Jesus said you should not worry about anything, that you should cast all your cares on Him so that He would carry them for you.

13. **Unwillingness to change and improve:** Paul says, "Study to show thyself approved."

John 13:26-28 says:

> *Jesus answered, He it is, to whom I shall give a sop, when I have dipped it. And when he had dipped the sop, he gave it to Judas Iscariot, the son of Simon. And after the sop Satan entered into him. Then said Jesus unto him, That thou doest, do quickly. Now no man at the table*

knew for what intent he spake this unto him.

Satan entered into Judas in the presence of Jesus because there was a weakness in him. In His own mercy, God will make every effort to reveal your weaknesses to you. Another trouble with weaknesses is that anytime they are in your life the devil will assign somebody from hell fire to feed them. There was a weakness in the life of Samson and Delilah was sent from hell fire to exploit and feed on it.

Your weakness should not be pampered or handled with kid gloves. It has an agenda which is to take over your life and destroy it. The weakness in your life will bond you with the wrong people, just like the weakness in the life of Samson bonded him with Delilah.

The weakness in a person's life will separate him from the right people. When you are separated from the right people you will be destroyed. That is why the right time to destroy your weaknesses is at the initial stage. If you overcome them, God will give you an incredible key that will move you forward. You need to identify this living organism called weakness, bring it out and kill it. If you do not do that, you will remain at the bottom.

POWER TO ESCAPE POVERTY

What do you do to escape from being programmed into the bottom?

1. **Discover and determine where God is taking you.**
2. **Desire and pursue that goal vigorously.**
3. **Discipline yourself to achieve your goal.** Discipline yourself to be at the top in anything in life. Do not entangle yourself with spiritual nonentities. Be serious with the things of God and your work.
4. **Have diligence and determination.**
5. **Drive away the giants blocking your way.**

Prayer Points

1. By the power of the Holy Ghost and the power in the blood of Jesus, let every arrow of darkness go back to the sender.
2. I wipe off, every record of my name in the demonic realm with the blood of Jesus.

3. Every yoke of the oppressor, be broken by fire, in Jesus' name.

4. Let my name become hot coals of fire that cannot be bewitched by any form of occultism, in the name of Jesus.

5. Any power, consulting the sun, the moon and the stars against me, be disgraced, in the name of Jesus.

6. Holy Ghost, arise with Your weapons of war and destroy every habitation of darkness programmed against my progress, in the name of Jesus.

7. Every incantation and enchantment raised against me, be destroyed, in the name of Jesus.

8. Let every token of darkness assigned against me be destroyed by the fire of God, in the name of Jesus.

9. I shall not die but live to declare the work of the Lord, in the name of Jesus.

10. Let every power of magic and soccery designed against me backfire, in the name of Jesus.

CHAPTER THREE

DIVINE VISITATION

The spiritual controls the physical; in the spiritual lies the power. In life, you can only have two types of visitation: physical and spiritual.

Divine visitation: Beloved, the truth is that, if God appears in your home, there would be peace there. If He appears in your business you will experience prosperity. If He appears to you in sickness, the sickness would fly away. If He appears to a demon-possessed he is set free. If He visits you, it is more than gathering all the General Overseers and prophets in this world into your sitting room. If He talks to you for five minutes it is more than any preacher talking to you for five years.

When you encounter divine visitation, it would give rise to unforgettable experiences, and uncommon breakthroughs and to your receiving priceless information and direction for your life. Beloved, it is indeed a wonderful thing to experience divine visitation. Divine visitation is when heavenly visitors pay you a visit. The house where they visit you in is blessed. If ou were sleeping on a bed that time the bed and pillow are blessed.

God is not a time-waster and does not pay purposeless visits. Enoch received many divine visitations and when the visitations became almost an everyday affair, God decided to take him to heaven.

Many complain day and night that they do not have uncommon breakthroughs. All that such people need to ask for is a divine visitation. When God appears in your situation, no matter how tough your enemies are, that is the day they will flee. No matter the battle you are fighting the battle ends when God appears at the war front.

WHEN GOD APPEARS

When God appeared to Noah, he was able to build the Ark. When He appeared to Jacob he was totally changed. When He appeared to Isaiah for the first time, Isaiah saw himself as he really was and said, "Woe is me for I am a man of unclean lips." For the first time he was able to locate himself. When He appeared to Jeremiah he received a wonderful commission which was to root up, to set up, to build and to plant. God's visitation to you has nothing to do with your age. If He appears to the aged, teenagers or young people, they will live completely different lives.

When God appeared to Paul he became the apostle to the gentiles. When He appeared to the parents of Samson they conceived Samson. When He appeared to Zachariah and Elizabeth they give birth to John. When He appeared to Prophet Elijah, for the first time Elijah could stand on Mount Carmel and challenge 850 prophets of Baal to a contest. It is therefore a very wonderful thing to receive a divine visitation. In this visitation, God would tell you things He would not tell others. It is an experience to be cherished.

Job 23:3-10 says:

> *Oh that I knew where I might find him! that I might come even to his seat! I would order my cause before him, and fill my mouth with arguments. I would know the words which he would answer me, and*

understand what he would say unto me. Will he plead against me with his great power? No; but he would put strength in me. There the righteous might dispute with him; so should I be delivered for ever from my judge. Behold, I go forward, but he is not there; and backward, but I cannot perceive him: On the left hand, where he doth work, but I cannot behold him: he hideth himself on the right hand, that I cannot see him: But he knoweth the way that I take: when he hath tried me, I shall come forth as gold.

Many believers know the Lord only superficially, but the Bible says, "They that know their God shall be strong." The opposite is that they that do not know their God shall be weak. Such people may know the General Overseer or any prophet, but that is different from knowing God. They that know their God shall do exploits and they that do not know their God shall be exploited.

Many do not really know God because they are seeking His hands but are not looking at His face. They find the time they spend in the presence of God completely uninteresting. Our present generation does not provide for quietness. But the secret many believers do not know is that the Lord loves to commune with us in quiet environment. He wants men to be His lover but when they have no time to hear from Him, it would be very difficult for Him to visit them. This is not just running to the mountain to encounter Him.

Many ran to the mountain with the problem of the valley and came back the same. You cannot force God to visit you. He will visit at His own time. For how long have you waited on Him for His visitation? When He appears in your blood your blood is charged. When He appears in that business all those swallowing it will run away and prosperity will come. When He appears in your spiritual life and you receive a divine visitation, you will become an entirely different person. As many people as are clamouring for a divine visitation and are thirsty and hungry for it should take this prayer point fervently.

God of Abraham, Isaac and Israel, visit me by fire, in the name of Jesus.

Somebody told me that he went on a 40 day fasting and the day he broke the fast he heard a voice which called his name and told him that he had failed. Failed after 40 days? This brother broke down and cried. This was a visitation of darkness. Sometimes people are told that demonic agents come to people and go away without harming them. This is a lie.

Whenever they visit, they plant invisible, evil materials in the body. There is practically no one who has not experienced any demonic visitation. If instead of moving forward you find yourself going backward it means you have experienced an evil visit which has prospered.

If you merit success but it is not coming your way, if you should be a winner but you are failing, if sometimes you don't even understand yourself, if there is a sudden hatred between you and your husband or wife, if you were a rich person but you are suddenly going poor,   if your life has remained completely stagnant for years, if you are feeling unnatural movements in parts of the body, if you are unable to receive the baptism of the Holy Ghost, if problems are just multiplying, all these mean that you have received an evil visitation and it prospered.

I pray that if evil visitation has prospered in your life, it shall be destroyed, in the name of Jesus.

Many have received body arrows during evil visitations and they begin to notice weakness in prayer, constant sickness, spiritual sluggishness, being fed regularly in he dream, inability to sleep well, sleeping during prayers, etc. They need to shake off this demonic arrows and command them to go back to where they came from.

EVIL VISITORS
I know a man of God whom a demon idol was sent to. He simply looked at the demon idol and smiled. The

demon idol came and stood before him and mentioned
all the names they gave the man on his ceremonial
naming day. First of all, the man of God instructed the
demon idol to stand at attention like a soldier and then
asked it what was in its hand. It said it was a club. The
man of God commanded it to hit the club on its head
and it obeyed. As he was hitting its head a woman's
voice was crying. The hitting continued until it broke its
head completely.

The next morning five people were dead. They were
those who conspired to send the evil visitor. I decree
that powers that have conspired to send evil visitors to
you shall receive their arrow back seven-fold, in the
name of Jesus.

THE MYSTERY

There is a mystery behind evil visitation which is
what we call the magnet of darkness. During such a
visit, the enemy deposits a tangible object which is
visible or invisible in the person's body. You can have a
plantation of darkness in your body. This is not just a
demon but a property of darkness. It is a negative
magnet. When it is in a person's body it would bring bad

luck and such a person would become a candidate of constant attacks. There would be blockage and unexplainable hatred, ˙terrible accidents and unexpected tragedies. This is why one has to be very careful.

A MAGNET

Once you acquire a magnet of darkness, it is like you're putting a dried fish and sugar inside your cupboard and you say that ants should not go there. Of course, the fish and the sugar would magnetise the ants and the rats. I decree that whatsoever is attracting the enemy to your life shall die, in the name of Jesus. If you go to a fake church and they bathe you or see visions for you, it is a magnet of darkness. If their prophets have slept with you, then you are in a big trouble. It is a magnet of darkness.

There are many things that can consume that magnet but first of all, we need to cry to God to forgive us of any sin that is bringing that magnet. We should repent our sins to the Lord and get saved. Then we should begin to clear out every evil property from our lives. Then we should cancel whatsoever the evil visitation has planted in our lives. Satan can never defeat a soul that is wearing the whole armour of God. He who wears the armour of God shall defeat satan. If you read your Bible very well, you will discover that there is no saint harassed by the enemy that did not come out victorious.

Genesis 3:14-16 says:

> *And the LORD God said unto the serpent, Because thou hast done this, thou art cursed above all cattle, and above every beast of the field; upon thy belly shalt thou go, and dust shalt thou eat all the days of thy life: And I will put enmity between thee and the woman, and between thy seed and her seed; it shall bruise thy head, and thou shalt bruise his heel. Unto the woman he said, I will greatly multiply thy sorrow and thy conception; in sorrow thou shalt bring forth children; and thy desire*

shall be to thy husband, and he shall rule over thee.

God has placed a curse on Satan to prostrate under our feet. And Jesus says that nothing shall by any means hurt us. For all the bruises that Satan is giving us by his visitation, he shall be rewarded with the breaking of his own head. As believers we are not food for the devil's mouth. For every weapon the devil has, God has a greater weapon and He will pursue our enemies and break their heads.

Those who are trying to destroy you shall help you to fulfil your destiny, in the name of Jesus. Whatever game the enemy has played so far, God would outplay him. God will take the clever hunter and put him in his own trap. He can arrange excellent deliverance for anybody. If He is working in your life no one can stop Him. We need to pray preventive, creative and defensive prayers to free ourselves.

Prayer Points

1. O Lord, make a way in my wilderness and provide rivers in my desert, in the name of Jesus.

2. Thou power of The Highest, overshadow my life, in Jesus' name.

3. Thou miracle-working power of the Most High God, begin full-time manifestation in my life now, in the name of Jesus.

4. My life and my destiny, reject bewitchment, in the name of Jesus.

5. Every power raising and strengthening dead problems in my life, die, in the name of Jesus.

6. My Father, turn the wisdom of my enemies to foolishness, in the name of Jesus.

7. My Father, turn the joy of the enemy over my life to sorrow, in the name of Jesus.

8. O Lord, cause my life to reflect You forever, in the name of Jesus.

9. Blood of Jesus, speak instant and permanent solution to my problems, in the name of Jesus.

10. Fire of the Holy Ghost, barricade my life and my family, in the name of Jesus.

CHAPTER FOUR

THE PROSPERITY MINDSET

You need a positive mindset to prosper in life.

YOUR THOUGHT CONTENTS

Thoughts can be a blessing; can also be a curse, depending on their contents. You and you alone can determine the contents of your thought. Technically or scripturally speaking, your mouth is either your best friend or your worst enemy, depending on how you use it. The Bible says, "As a man thinketh in his heart, so is he." It is sin that has produced the carnal mind people have now. Man was put in the Garden of Eden with an innocent mind, with no thoughts of evil at all. Satan tempted man and told him that God lied to him. He duped man and then the carnal mind took over. When the Lord saw that the wickedness of man was great, He decided to sweep him away with the flood.

Sometimes, when you begin to read the New Testaments, especially where the Bible says, "Think not that....." Jesus thought us how to think, He also thought us how not to think. Wrong and right thinking matters.

Wrong thinking has to be removed in order for right thinking to take over. If you want to change your surroundings and your life, start inside. When you make the right changes in your thinking, other things will turn out right in your life.

YOUR FOCUS

When you change the thinking of your mind, you change your focus. When you are able to change that focus, you change your destiny. Right thinking, however, is difficult, especially if a person has been used to thinking evil, thinking bad. How can somebody be standing at the bus-stop and be thinking that a bus would just run over his or her leg there? When a thought pattern has been going on for years it becomes what the Bible calls a stronghold. There is no accidental fornication or adultery. It is not possible. It has been in your thoughts. You have been meditating upon it all this while.

Proverb 4:23 says:

Keep thy heart with all diligence; for out of it are the issues of life.

Romans 8:6 says:

> *For to be carnally minded is death;*
> *but to be spiritually minded is life*
> *and peace.*

You must be spiritually minded if you want life. You alone know what you are thinking now. What occupies your daily thoughts most? I ask this question today because the Bible says there is a direct relationship between what you are thinking today and the kind of person you will be tomorrow. Are your thoughts good or bad? Negative or positive? Godly or ungodly. You are what you think. What you are today is what you thought yesterday.

1 Peter 1:13 says:

> *Wherefore gird up the loins of your*
> *mind, be sober, and hope to the end*
> *for the grace that is to be brought unto*
> *you at the revelation of Jesus Christ.*

The loin is the reproductive area of the human body. Our mind is the reproductive area of our spirits and must be guarded with the word of God and the Holy Ghost. Sin is a result of bad thoughts. Your thought life is the beginning of victory in your life. It is also the beginning of defeat, depending on what you are thinking.

A WARPED MENTALITY

Sometime ago, I said that those who never entered the Promise Land had mind problems. They saw themselves as grasshoppers. But those like Joshua and Caleb, who saw themselves in the Promised Land in their minds, got there. The bones of Joseph got to the Promised Land because he saw them there, but those who carried the bones died in the wilderness. When you have the mind of victory, you become victorious. When you have the mind of power, you become powerful. If you read the book of Psalms very well, you will discover that David made music part of everything he experienced. He saw every adversity as something that had an alternative. He had a winning mentality. There is nowhere in the Bible that it is stated that light should run away when it sees darkness. I pray that you will run towards your Goliath as David did, in the name of

Jesus. And I pray that your Goliath shall be disgraced, in Jesus' name.

Jeremiah 17:9 says:

> *The heart is deceitful above all things, and desperately wicked: who can know it?*

DECEIVED HEARTS

The heart is deep and desperately wicked. As a man thinketh in his heart so is he. A man of God was preaching about hell fire and right there in front of the congregation was a woman weeping profusely. After the service he beckoned on her to pray for her, telling her that God could forgive all sins. But she was still weeping profusely and she asked the pastor why he didn't ask her why she was crying. Then the pastor asked and she said it was because she wished the handsome pastor were her husband. The pastor jumped out of his seat in shock. Here was a woman weeping for such an issue when a message on "The Mind and Hell fire" was going on.

THE CONTROL CENTRE

"Above all things keep your heart with all diligence, for out of it are the issues of life." You may not be able to stop a bird from flying over your head, but you are able to stop it from building a nest on your head. All you need to do is to blow it off your head. You may not be able to stop the devil from bringing evil suggestions to you, but you can lock them out. A new mind creates a new life. Righteousness in your mind brings out beauty in your character. When you are intellectually educated, you have an intellectual culture, but with a bad heart you are a civilised barbarian. To change your character and your life, you must begin at the control centre which is your heart.

This is a serious matter. The heart is deep, wicked, deceitful and can fail us. It can be proud, it can be like a wax, be at war within itself and can imagine mischief. It can be perverse, sick, without hope and secretly enticed. The heart can be hard and adamant and can be mad. There are plenty of mad hearts around. Plenty of the so-called decent people in Nigeria are decently mad.

THE CHARACTERISTICS

The heart can be lustful, slow, blind, wounded and can backslide. It can be hypocritical, fat and greasy. It can be desolate, despising, bitter and foolish. It can be in error, abominable, not being penitent and doubtful. It can be stony, strange, troubled and darkened. It grieves God when our heart is dark and is pushing us away from Him. The heart is the place of encounter with God.

What then is the condition of your heart?

What kind of thoughts do you allow? Have you succeeded in blocking evil thoughts out of your heart?

It is when terrible things are crossing through the heart that one day the person would develop a spiritual heart attack. When this happens the blood vessels in the heart become hardened. When your heart becomes hardened, spiritual heart attack occurs.

THE ANOINTED

The kind of heart that God wants is the anointed mind. You need to cry to heavens for God to anoint your heart. The Psalmist says, "Let the word of my mouth and the meditations of my heart be acceptable in thy sight, O Lord."

An anointed mind is a mind that meditates according ton Philipians 4:8 which says:

> *Finally, brethren, whatsoever things are true, whatsoever things are honest, whatsoever things are just, whatsoever things are pure, whatsoever things are lovely, whatsoever things are of good report; if there be any virtue, and if there be any praise, think on these things.*

POSITIVE THOUGHTS

The anointed mind only thinks of what is in the above passage. Anything outside this is an ugly mind, an un-anointed mind and the mind is focused on hell fire. An anointed mind is a mind that is humble. When you overrate yourself it is pride and you are crying for a fall. An anointed mind is a mind that is not conformed to this world. It is a mind that is renewed and renovated. When your mind is conformed to the world it is not anointed. An anointed mind is a mind that is always positive. An anointed mind is a mind that is set on things above, a disciplined mind that is continually being renewed. Remember that life and death are issues that come from the mind. It is written "Above all things keep your heart with all diligence for out of it are the issues of life."

Prayer Points

1. Lord, let Your miracle be stretched out upon my life now.
2. Lord, let Your hand of deliverance be stretched out upon my life now.
3. I disannul every engagement with the spirit of death, in Jesus' name.
4. I rebuke every refuge of sickness, in the name of Jesus.
5. I destroy the grip and operation of sickness upon my life, in the name of Jesus.
6. Every knee of infirmity in my life, bow, in the name of Jesus.

7. Lord, let my negativity be converted to positivity, in the name of Jesus.

8. I command death upon .any sickness in any area of my life, in the name of Jesus.

9. I shall see my sickness no more, in the name of Jesus.

10. Father Lord, let Your whirlwind scatter every vessel of infirmity fashioned against my life, in the name of Jesus.

11. Every spirit hindering my perfect healing, fall down and die now, in the name of Jesus.

12. Father Lord, let all death contractors begin to kill themselves, in the name of Jesus.

13. Father Lord, let every germ of infirmity in my body die, in the name of Jesus.

14. Father Lord, let every agent of sickness working against my health disappear, in the name of Jesus.

CHAPTER FIVE

ENVIRONMENTAL FACTORS

Some environmental factors are responsible for poverty or prosperity. When you take environmental factors into consideration, you will find it easy to possess your possession in the area of wealth and prosperity. When the nation prospers, individuals will also prosper. The prosperity of Nigeria is the foundation of your prosperity, if you are a Nigerian.

Psalm 122:6 says:

> *Pray for the peace of Jerusalem: they shall prosper that love thee.*

All over the world, Nigeria is known as a unique nation. Barring the negative image carved by a few bad eggs, It remains a country that is unique in every sense. Viewed from many angles, Nigeria is a blessed nation. Nigeria has raised world class scientists, produced world class businessmen, presented exceptional sportsmen and women and created a record that is difficult to be broken in religion in the world.

EXCEPTIONAL SKILLS

People from advanced countries have identified the exceptional skills of many Nigerians. They have grown to respect the skills and the abilities of the Nigerians that have proved themselves exceptional. The only problem is that some Nigerians have pushed their skills to the realm of notoriety. Rather than use such skills positively, some have used them negatively.

In Cameroon, for example, there is a common saying. that it is only a Nigerian woman that has the guts to slap her husband. Beyond the negative tag, it is very clear that God has given Nigerians the intelligence to produce exceptional and creative things.

A SPECIAL BREED

There was a programme on a foreign television sometime ago which centred on the greatest nations of the world. It was a comparative analysis of the skills of nationalities of all the countries in the world. When mention was made of Nigeria, a white man uttered the timeless words that as far as he was concerned, God created three kinds of people: the whites, the blacks and the Nigerians. This shows that Nigerians are a special breed of people.

There was a common joke among the British police. If a Nigerian is arrested, don't ever give him time to think. If you give him time to think, he will surely outsmart you. Laws and codes of conduct are brought out in many countries of the world and respected. In fact, in some countries to think of breaking the law is actually unthinkable. But what nations bring up as barriers can remain so only when a Nigerian has not showed up. If you create the highest barrier, when a Nigerian shows up, within 10 minutes, he will either dismantle it, find a way round it, or escape outrightly.

MODELS OF EXCELLENCE

Nigerians have become models of creative excellence. With the breed of people that Nigeria has been endowed with, it is crystal clear that God has a unique destiny for Nigeria. He cannot give us the best skills, the best brains, the best business acumen and the best talents just to make us remain at the tail region. He has given us excellent resources because He wants to make the Nigerian nation a paragon of excellence.

Take a look at the Church, God has hand-picked respected Nigerian professionals, scientists, scholars and those who have proved themselves in their chosen fields to lift up the banner of Christ. A good number of churches have been able to exert positive influence on the elite class. In other words, if you take an inventory of the number of important personalities who attend gospel or Pentecostal churches, you would discover that God has a purpose for Nigeria. Take a look at Africa and you will discover that the missionary force that has turned the continent around has been raised predominantly by Nigeria. There is hardly any nation on earth today where Nigerians have not carried or is not carrying out missionary activities.

Several years ago, missionaries came from Europe and America to Nigeria. Today, Nigeria is fast dominating the scenes of missionary activities. At home and abroad, Nigerians are raising the largest churches, all of these point to the fact that God has an agenda for Nigeria.

Go to any part of the globe, you will surely find a Nigerian there. Among the Asians, in cold regions like

Iceland, in far flung places like South America, even in countries where the language spoken is difficult to understand, you will find Nigerians there. If you gather six Africans together, one of them must be a Nigerian. Undoubtedly, Nigeria is a nation of destiny.

THE TRIGGER

When the colonial masters came, they surely did not know that God had deposited much more than they could ever imagine among the people that make up Nigeria. If you take a discerning look at the map of Africa, you will discover that it looks like a gun. Importantly, Nigeria is located at the place where the trigger is found. This shows that Nigeria is the trigger of the African continent. Gather the news items of the African continent together, you will discover that the headlines are pointing to the going-on in Nigeria.

Nigeria is a country of resources. It is amazing that there is hardly any prominent natural resource that is not found in Nigeria. If you take crude oil as an example, you will discover that Nigeria is one of the top world producers. In fact, the Nigerian crude oil, ranks as one of the best in the world. Nigeria also has the largest deposit of bitumen in the world. What is more, there is a wonderful array of human resources. Nigerian scientists are of world class. They compare favourably with their counterparts in other parts of the world. Interestingly, the man who manufactured the fastest computer in the world is a Nigerian, Philip Emegwali.

AN INDISPENSABLE BREED

Nigerians are very intelligent. We are undisputably one of the smartest peoples of the world. In places like Saudi Arabia and the whole of Arab Emirates, there are exceptional Nigerian geologists and engineers carrying out invaluable services. If someone were to evacuate all Nigerians from all countries of the world, a lot of things would go wrong. The countries will suddenly lack the man-power needed for their economy, science and technology, the IT, commerce, sports and other fields of human endeavour. God has placed in Nigerian nation, people who have exceptional skills, very high intelligence quotient, incomparable skills, uncommon perseverance, unique knack for hard work and abilities that are rare.

THE HAPPIEST NATION

Several years ago when I was still an employee of the Nigerian Medical Research Institute, I got to know of a research that was made concerning the entire globe. Its thrust was to find out how happy the citizens of various countries were. By the time the researchers came up with their result, they discovered that Nigeria came first. In other words, Nigerians are the happiest people on earth. The second country whose citizens were on the happy people's chart was Venezuela. Nigerians proved to the whole world that in spite of their economic problems, political instability, unprecedented job cuts, unemployment, etc, they have remained happy.

If what has happened to citizens of Nigeria had happened to members of other countries, such people would have ran berserk. God has, no doubt, made Nigerians a unique breed. The fact that they are the happiest people in the world, according to the research, threw many people off balance. Some Nigerians wondered why people who could be adjudged poor by world standards could be happy. Someone has humorously stated that the best words that can be used to describe Nigerians are the words of a late musician who said that Nigerians were suffering and smiling.

THE INVISIBLE HAND

Beloved, the Nigerian nation has a destiny. What has happened in Nigeria and what some Nigerians have done to keep the nation apart would have divided some other countries to 10 splinter nations. Whenever something sad happens in Nigeria, sections of the country would come up with threats of secession. But such threats have not seen the light of day because God has laid his hands upon Nigeria. Sometimes, the newspapers carry stories of massive importation of arms. Even if such news were true, Nigeria has survived its consequences. There is an invisible hand holding Nigeria together because of the divine role it has been ordained to play.

In view of the diversity of the over 362 languages or dialects, spoken in Nigeria, one would marvel at our unity in diversity. Again, when you look at the efforts by some ethnic groups to dominate the nation, you would wonder why the nation has not fallen apart. What with the agitations of the minority tribes. There has been lots of uprisings. Militant groups have made spirited efforts to make the nation ungovernable, but God has kept Nigeria on the level of stability.

THE ENDURANCE LEVEL

The endurance level of Nigerians is simply incomparable. If you want to know the people who can take up multiple jobs in different parts of the world, you simply have to locate Nigerians. No matter the barriers erected in many nations, it is difficult to wear Nigerians out. The citizens of those countries may go about whining and complaining but Nigerians will simply sit down and evolve methods aimed at beating the barriers. They have evinced uncommon resilience, perseverance and skills that know no impossibility.

It is interesting that, most of the best pilots and scientists in the world are from Nigeria. Anywhere you go, you will find a Nigerian speaking, either Igbo, Hausa or Yoruba. Nigerians own exotic and exquisite shops abroad. The institutions of higher learning abroad are filled by Nigerian students and lecturers. Nigerians have become professors of American literature, Hispanic studies and British History. They have been able to go to places where languages like Spanish, German and French are spoken and have become professors of such languages. No doubt, Nigerians have earned the admiration of people from advanced countries of the world.

SATANIC DEVICES

However, the devil had planned lots of casualties for Nigeria, but God has frustrated its plans. Even when some personalities have tried to sell Nigeria spiritually to the altar of witchcraft, politics, cultism, money rituals and sectional mafia, God has continued to have His way. It is indeed true as recorded in Proverbs 19:21 that:

> *There are many devices in a man's heart; nevertheless the counsel of the LORD, that shall stand.*

And Daniel 4:35 says:

> *And all the inhabitants of the earth are reputed as nothing: and he doeth*

according to his will in the army of heaven, and among the inhabitants of the earth: and none can stay his hand, or say unto him, What doest thou?

God has therefore vowed to contend with those who contend with the destiny of Nigeria. Those who have constituted themselves as eaters of flesh and drinkers of blood of Nigeria shall be made to drink their own blood and eat their own flesh according to the Psalm 27:2 which says:

When the wicked, even mine enemies and my foes, came upon me to eat up my flesh , they stumbled and fell.

Isaiah 49:26 also says:

And I will feed them that oppress thee with their own flesh ; and they shall be drunken with their own blood, as with sweet wine: and all flesh shall know

that I the LORD am thy Saviour and
thy Redeemer, the mighty One of Jacob.

GOD'S DIVINE PLAN

The judgment of God will continue to be heated up
against those who stand on His way of glorious agenda
for Nigeria. God has predetermined the boundaries of
Nigeria. The boundaries will remain intact according to
God's agenda. Although Nigeria is the largest black
nation on earth with uncommon diversity, yet God has
decided to have His way according to Act 17:26 which
says:

And hath made of one blood all nations
of men for to dwell on all the face of the
earth, and hath determined the times
before appointed, and the bounds of
their habitation.

Let all those who have hidden agenda for Nigeria
beware. No one can contest with the Almighty and win.
No political power can derail God's plan. No political
godfather can toy with a nation established by God. If

evil men should venture to carry out their evil plans, they will pay dearly for it. Pray for Nigeria and you shall also prosper.

Prayer Points
1. All environmental planners of evil, scatter, in Jesus' name.
2. My spirit-man, arise by the fire and thunder of God and disgrace every tragedy activator working against me, in the name of Jesus.
3. I refuse to be a victim for eaters of flesh and drinkers of blood, in the name of Jesus.
4. My blood shall not be available on any altar of satan, in Jesus' name.
5. I shall run and not be weary, and walk and not faint, in Jesus' name.
6. Every power planning tragedy for me, be disgraced, in Jesus' name.
7. Every conspiracy against my wellbeing, melt away, in Jesus' name.
8. Power of God, move against every witchcraft attack working against me, in the name of Jesus.
9. God, arise and let all the enemies of my peace scatter, in the name of Jesus.

10. By the power of the Holy Ghost, I arise to overcome every environmental serpent and scorpion, in the name of Jesus.

11. God that sitteth in the heavens, laugh to scorn every power conspiring against my life, in the name of Jesus.

12. Anything in my life that would remove my shield of protection, be destroyed, in the name of Jesus.

OTHER BOOKS BY DR. D. K. OLUKOYA

YORUBA PUBLICATIONS

FRENCH PUBLICATIONS

11. Prieres Violentes Pour Humilier Les Problsmes Opiniatres
12. Priere Pour Detruire Les Maladies Et Les Infirmites
13. Le Combat Spirituel Et Le Foyer
14. Bilan Spirituel Personnel
15. Victoires Sur Les Reves Sataniques
16. Prieres De Combat Contre 70 Esprits Dechalnes
17. La Deviation Satanique De La Race Noire
18. Ton Combat Et Ta Strategie
19. Votre Fondement Et Votre Destin
20. Revoquer Les Decrets Malefiques
21. Cantique Des Coritiques
22. Le Mauvais Cri Des Idoles
23. Quand Les Choses Deviennent Difficiles
24. Les Strategies De Prieres Pour Les Celibataires
25. Se Liberer Des Alliances Malefiques
26. Demanteler La Sorcellerie
27. La Deliverance: Le Flacon De Medicament De Dieu
28. La Deliverance De La Tete
29. Commander Le Matin
30. Ne Grand Mais Lie
31. Pouvoir Contre Les Demons Tropicaux
32. Le Programme De Tranfert Des Rlchesse
33. Les Etudiants A l'ecole De La Peur
34. L'etoile Dans Votre Ciel
35. Les Saisons De La Vie
36. Femme Tu Es Liberee

ALL OBTAINABLE AT:

The Battle Cry Christian Ministries-
322, Herbert Macaulay Street, Sabo, Yaba.
P. O. Box 12272, Ikeja, Lagos
Telephone: 08033044239, 01-8044415

MFM International Bookshop
13, Olasimbo Street, Onike-Yaba, Lagos

IPEY Music Konnections Limited -
48, Opebi Road, Salvation Bus-Stop
(234-47194971, 234-8033056093)

All MFM Church Branches nationwide
and leading Christian Bookstores

BOOK ORDER

Is there any book by
Dr. D. K. Olukoya
(General Overseer MFM Ministries)
that you would like to have?

Have you seen his latest books?
To place an order for this End-Time Materials,
Call: 08161229775

Battle Cry Ministries... Equipping the saints of God.

God bless.

Made in the USA
Columbia, SC
26 November 2019

83875007R00046